I0117304

Developing Oneness In Marriage

A "How-to" for Husbands

By the Rev. Dr. Lloyd C. Blue

Searchlight Press
Dallas, Texas

Developing Oneness
in Marriage:

A "How-to" for Husbands

by the Reverend Doctor Lloyd C. Blue

ISBN #: 978-1-936497-06-5

©2011, Lloyd C. Blue

Searchlight Press
Who are you looking for?
Publishers of thoughtful Christian books since 1994.
5634 Ledgestone Drive
Dallas, TX 75214-2026
888.896.6081
info@Searchlight-Press.com
www.Searchlight-Press.com

Manufactured in the United States of America

Dedication

I dedicate this book to my darling wife (Tressie).

Honey, I need you like the river needs the water. Thank you for being there for me these fifty-five years. You are indeed a virtuous wife, always seeking ways to support our son (Lloyd) and me. There is no way I could have found a better person to love forever.

LCB

TABLE OF CONTENTS

WHO SHOULD READ THIS BOOK

This book, **Developing Oneness in Marriage**, is recommended reading for men of any age group, no matter what race, creed or color.

First, this is a must read for husbands whether you have been married for a short time or soon to be fifty-six years, as I have.

Secondly, it is for single men who desire God to provide for them just the right mate, because God only provides when we give him a reason.

Thirdly, it is for pastors. **Developing Oneness in Marriage** is a teaching, training and counseling tool.

In closing, I recommend the use of this book for anyone involved in leading, instructing or counseling men.

LCB

FOREWORD

Dr. Lloyd Blue has my genuine respect when it comes to ministering in the area of marriage and relationships.

This book is a testimony to his successful marriage of fifty-five years and the numerous couples he has counseled during his forty-nine years of ministry. His scripture-based advice on how to have a flourishing marriage is priceless and should be included in every ministerial library.

I would recommend **Developing Oneness in Marriage: A "How-to" for Husbands** to anyone currently married, desiring to be married or wanting to teach the principles of solid relationships. With the God-ordained institution of marriage being assaulted, divorce rates increasing, and many of our young people believing that "shacking up" is the obvious precursor to marriage, it is time for a book that teaches young and old alike what it takes to have a marriage that honors God and His word.

This mighty man of God, who is a loving husband and father, has taken time to show the applicable scriptures, which will enlighten, edify and enhance the union between a man and a woman. Although this book is scripturally and doctrinally sound, the non-believer can easily apply his instructions and be all the better for having taken the time to listen to this sage advice.

If anyone is lacking in wisdom in the area of marriage, here is your chance to increase or achieve the knowledge you may desperately need. This theologian has blessed my marriage of thirty-four years and I know this book will be a blessing to you as well.

You did not pick up this book by accident, it was meant for you! Read **Developing Oneness in Marriage: A "How-to" for Husbands**, and be blessed!

Dr. Wm. Dwight McKissic, Sr.
Pastor of Cornerstone Baptist Church
Arlington, Texas

INTRODUCTION

Because the Bible teaches oneness, we must all strive for oneness, especially husbands and wives. Listen now to...

THE PRAYER FOR ONENESS
AS PRAYED BY OUR LORD
John 17:11, 21

[11] Now I am no longer in the world, but these are in the world, and I come to You. Holy Father, keep through Your name those whom You have given Me, that they may be one as We *are*.

Jesus prayed that we might be one as He and the Father are one. What a great goal to set for our marriages.

[21] that they all may be one, as You, Father, *are* in Me, and I in You; that they also may be one in Us, that the world may believe that You sent Me.

To have oneness with our wives, we both must have oneness with the Father and the Son. But there is also...

THE POWER OF ONENESS
Matthew 18:20

[20] For where two or three are gathered together in My name, I am there in the midst of them."

Here, Jesus promises that when you and your wife are living in oneness, in His name, He will be present.

Let's look for just a moment at what the Bible teaches us about marriage.

Marriage is God's idea: *"A man leaves his mother and father and is joined to his wife, and the two are united as one."* (Genesis 2:24)

Jesus referring back to this passage added, *"Since they are no longer two but one, let no one separate them, for God has joined them together."* (Matthew 19:5)

Marriage is a metaphor for the relationship between Christ and the church. We read in Ephesians 5:31-32, *"A man leaves his father and mother and is joined to his wife, and the two are united as one. This is a great mystery, but it is an illustration of the way Christ and the church are one."*

God-honoring marriages with Christ at the center will point the world to the kind of relationship God wants to have with every person! Your marriage is to be a testimony to the world of the love of Christ and the faithfulness of God!

Marriage is to be a life-long pursuit of oneness.

Right now in the United States one-third of all first marriages will end in divorce and nearly fifty percent of all married people will experience at least one divorce. And that percentage is the same for those who profess to be born-again Christians.

> **Being a Christian doesn't guarantee a trouble free marriage; instead it's all the more reason for a commitment on our part to a life-long pursuit of oneness.**

What that tells me is, as Christians, we are in no way immune to the pain and reality of divorce. Being a Christian doesn't guarantee a trouble free marriage; instead it's all the more reason for a commitment on our part to a life-long pursuit of oneness. We need to be praying for our married brothers and sisters in Christ.

What does it mean to strive for "oneness" in the Biblical sense? This is a little tricky because we tend, in our culture, to equate feelings with love. We've been taught that love is something we "feel" toward the other. As long as we feel loving toward each other in our marriage, we're okay.

But what happens when I lose the feeling of love, even temporarily? Like when I'm so focused on myself, and my needs, and I completely neglect her? How do you feel love toward someone so unlovely?

Oneness, which is healthy and biblical, may begin with "feeling" love but it grows from there. It requires both action and sacrifice. I want to share with you what I have learned over the past fifty-four years to be the **B.E.S.T.** way to nurture oneness:

$\underline{B}$- Bless your wife.
"Bless" means, "to speak well of."

Proverbs 15:23 says, *"Everyone enjoys a fitting reply; it is wonderful to say the right thing at the right time!"*

We tend to do this well when we're first dating. We can't say enough good things to and about each other. What we can't say face to face we write in mushy love letters.

1. Speak well of your wife to friends and family.
2. Speak well to your wife in casual conversation and in arguments.
3. Speak well of your wife through action – "Action speaks louder than words." (Flowers, cards, letters, gifts, weekend getaways, etc.)

$\underline{E}$- Encourage your wife.
"Encourage" means "to build up."

"Let everything you say be good and helpful, so that your words will be an encouragement to those who hear them." (Ephesians 4:29)

Sometimes it's much easier to build up a friend, a colleague or even a complete stranger than it is to build up our wives. We should be our wife's greatest cheerleaders!

$\underline{S}$- Submit to your wife.
"Submit" means "to refer (respect)."

If there's ever been a scripture that gives us trouble, it's Ephesians 5 where Paul talks about husbands being the head of his wife and wife submitting to her husband. Unfortunately, we want to move right past verse 21 to get to that good stuff. Paul writes in verse 21, *"You will submit yourself to one another out of reverence for Christ."* And in verse 33, *"each man must love his wife as he loves himself, and the wife must respect her husband."*

Oneness is mutual submission! Men, we have to put to death our own selfish and egocentric traits to focus intently on the needs of our wives. I am sure we can agree, that for us men, to submit to our wives feels a lot like trying to breath underwater.

Although, we fight our natural tendency to be self-centered and self-indulgent, it's a real struggle for us because the media either paints us as bullies running wildly over our wives and children or as absolute buffoons who are clueless about everything!

T- Treasure your wife.
"Treasure" means "to value (cherish)."

A golden anniversary party was thrown to honor an elderly couple. The husband was so moved by the occasion, he wanted to tell his wife and all their guests just how he felt about her. She was very hard of hearing, however, and often had to have things repeated until she understood. The cheerful husband stood to toast his wife. "My dear wife, after fifty years I've found you tried and true!"

Everyone smiled. But his wife said, "Eh?" He repeated it loudly. "AFTER FIFTY YEARS OF MARRIAGE I'VE FOUND YOU TRIED AND TRUE!"

His wife harrumphed and shot back, "Well, let me tell you something mister—after fifty years I'm tired of you too!"

Wouldn't it be great to get to fifty years still treasuring the gift God gave you in your wife? Who wouldn't want to experience such joy! It begins now by finding ways to cherish her.

Men, according to a recent survey, 84% of women feel they don't have intimacy (oneness) in their marriages. A large majority of female divorcees say their married years were the loneliest of their lives.
God has called us to love our wives as ourselves and to lay down our lives that we might be one with them.

Do you want to experience oneness in your marriage?

Bless your wife.
Tell her and others how much she means to you.
Encourage your wife.
Be her greatest cheerleader!
Submit yourself to her –
really wanting to put her needs above your own.
Treasure her –
as the gift God intended her to be in your life!

**THE PURPOSE OF THIS BOOK
IS TO HELP YOU GET FOCUSED
ON YOUR RESPONSIBILITY
AS A HUSBAND
AND TO CREATE ONENESS
IN YOUR MARRIAGE.**

Notes

Chapter One

MORE IMPORTANT!

YOU MUST REALIZE THAT ONE OF THE BASIC NEEDS OF YOUR WIFE IS TO SENSE THAT SHE IS VIEWED BY YOU AS MORE IMPORTANT THAN ANYTHING ELSE IN YOUR LIFE.

One way to meet this basic need is to provide adequate time for her. You must make her your number one priority. It will also help if you give her a big hug and kiss before leaving for work each day, and call her sometime during the day to tell her you love her and you are looking forward to being with her after work.

Some men work more than they must. They think, that getting "things" for their wife and children, they are doing the right thing, however, what the family really wants, is dad.

I have counseled a number of wives who would have gladly done without the bigger house, the bigger car, the bigger television etc. just to be able to spend time with their husbands. What good will it do you to work a job and a half, month after month, only to lose the very one for whom you have been working?

Some men are too involved in sports. The first thing they grab in the morning is the sports page. Jim Jones was just such a sports enthusiast. Each morning he would bury himself behind the sports page while eating his breakfast and drinking his coffee. No matter what she said, when Mrs. Jones would try to talk to him, all she could get out of him were grunts, groans, and occasional yep or some other inaudible sound.

Finally one morning, she trapped him by loudly saying, "I bet you don't know what day this is?"

Jim replied, "Of course I know what day this is? How could I forget?"

At noon she received a dozen roses with a card that read, "I love you, Happy Anniversary."

About three in the afternoon she received a heart shaped box of chocolates and another I love you happy anniversary card. About five o'clock, she received beautiful nightgown. When he arrived home about 6:00 PM his wife had cooked his favorite meal. When he walked through the door and smelled the food he said, "Honey you shouldn't have."

She replied, "I just couldn't help myself. After all, you have made this the most exciting Ground Hog Day I have ever experienced."

The moral of this story is, reading the sports page when your wife is trying to talk to you can be needlessly expensive. Some guys come home from work, eat and then go sit in front of the television. They watch the sports news, the pre-game show, the game and the post game wrap up. When this occurs, their wives spend another lonely night at home with their husbands in the house.

> To build oneness in marriage you have to spend quantity and quality time with her. Don't take your wife for granted.

A lot of women are complaining these days, about their husbands being addicted to CNN and the Internet. I have counseled people who have been divorced because of these addictions.

Then there are those who sleep too much. I counseled with a wife who told me her husband was in bed asleep by 8:30 PM and if she wanted sex she would have to wake him up. There was no foreplay, just on her for a minute or two and back to sleep.

To build oneness in marriage you have to spend quantity and quality time with her. Don't take your wife for granted. Time with her is not just desire, it's a need. She needs enough time to express her thoughts to you. Time with your wife is the best way to say, I LOVE YOU.

RELATED SCRIPTURE
Ephesians 5:25-29

Husbands, love your wives, just as Christ also loved the church and gave Himself for her, that He might sanctify and cleanse her with the washing of water by the word, that He might present her to Himself a glorious church, not having spot or wrinkle or any such thing, but that she should be holy and without blemish. So husbands ought to love their own wives as their own bodies; he who loves his wife loves himself. For no one ever hated his own flesh, but nourishes and cherishes it, just as the Lord does the church.

You must love your wife as Christ loved the church (v. 25); this is "agape" the highest kind of love. Meaning you must love her "sacrificially" just as Christ gave Himself for the church. This kind of love is motivated by what it can give and not by what it can get. You must love your wife as your own body, "nourishing" and "cherishing" her (v. 29).

To nourish means to provide for her just as you provide for your own body. Just as you provide food, water and medical care for your body, you must do the same for your wife and much more.

To cherish means to protect her just as you protect your own body. You will do what ever you have to do to protect your body from harm; using plain common sense, do likewise for your wife.

IF YOU REJECT THE ABOVE, YOU WILL CREATE THESE NEGATIVE CONSEQUENCES:

·   She feels insecure and unimportant.

·   She feels lonely even when she is in the company of others.

·   She feels incomplete without you.

·   She gives her life to you, thinking you're the one who loves her and wants to make her happy, and then begins to think you
don't love her that much.

·   She feels unloved (She feels she is unsupported and friendless and as a result
looks elsewhere for her needs to be net).

·   She feels deprived (She seeks attention from another male with whom she feels is able to provide her with communication and meet her real and felt needs.

Chapter Two

VALUE YOUR WIFE'S OPINION

YOU MUST VALUE
THE OPINIONS OF YOUR WIFE
AS MUCH AS YOU MERIT YOUR OWN.

The average man tends to think a woman's ideas are inferior. She is deeply hurt if her ideas are not considered or even heard. Even though her frame of reference is different from the man's, her opinions are just as valuable.

Very often the wife is a better judge of character due to her sensitivity to the spirit of a person. The husband tends to overlook character faults and concentrates on the logical nature of a person's ideas.

During the late 70's and early 80's I decided to get involved in real estate investments, something I knew nothing about. For the most part I ignored my wife and went full speed ahead. I even got others involved. To make a long story short I was not a victor and caused others to lose a lot of money. I learned my lesson.

Today, if I am going to make a business deal (large or small) I want my wife with me and I will not commit to anything until I have time to talk it over with my wife and get her opinion.

That took place about 35 years ago and since that time I have learned, while doing ministry to men, that some men have a problem listening to their wives' opinions. A wise husband will listen carefully to his wife and will consider the input she provides. He will not lightly nor casually dismiss her opinion.

I want to challenge husbands everywhere to listen carefully to their wives and humbly consider what they are saying.

The men at our church and at seminars I conduct across the country are beginning to value and listen to their wives. My wife has often provided me with a much needed prospective on issues that have helped me make better decisions or that has changed my thinking. She is my trusted counselor and my wise advisor. But after I have listened to her, she expects me to be the leader in our home. She wants me to be the one who is responsible before God for wise decision-making.

I want to challenge husbands everywhere to listen carefully to their wives and humbly consider what they are saying. This does not mean you wimp out and fail as God's leader in the home.

RELATED SCRIPTURE
1 Peter 3:7

Husbands, likewise, dwell with them with understanding, giving honor to the wife, as to the weaker vessel, and as being heirs together of the grace of life, that your prayers may not be hindered.

There is a serious gap in men's knowledge of women. Men, we must first read the Bible to see what God has to say about women and read other books like, <u>What Women Wish Their Husbands Knew about Them</u>.

We must also read books about sex, love and romance. Moreover, we need to spend time with them in conversation and ask questions. The more you learn about your wife the more prepared you will be to meet her needs.

IF YOU REJECT THE ABOVE, YOU WILL CREATE THESE NEGATIVE CONSEQUENCES:

- She feels an inward hurt. (It causes her deep emotional pain)
- She feels resentful. (She feels anger and vengeful)
- She lacks confidence that God even cares.
- She refuses to share ideas with you.

- She feels inferior and inadequate.
- She becomes reluctant to communicate. (She becomes afraid to give further opinions)

Notes

Chapter Three

A WIFE'S STRENGTHS

YOU MUST CONCENTRATE ON YOUR WIFE'S STRENGTHS, WHILE LOOKING FOR WAYS TO ENCOURAGE HER AND BUILD-UP HER INNER SPIRIT.

When you concentrate on her weaknesses and failures, you are communicating that you do not accept her as she is. Learn to look beyond your wife's faults and minister to her needs. The closer you get to her the more you will notice her imperfections. However, acceptance is looking past her faults and meeting her needs. Be especially sensitive to the fact that acceptance is a God-given need in the life of your wife.

Are you careless in the way you talk to your wife? It has been said in a book on marriage, "That It takes 100 compliments to balance out ONE criticism from a husband or wife."

I don't know about you, but I'd have trouble coming up with 100 compliments! It's a lot smarter – guys – to swallow the careless criticism! Remember this helpful quote from Winston Churchill. He once said, "By swallowing evil words unsaid, no one has ever harmed his stomach."

Concentrate on the positive. Rather than making insensitive and inappropriate attempts to change your wife, support her in prayer and be willing for God to do His work in her life. Ask God to help you see your wife as He sees her, and to love her as He commands you to love her. Don't expect her to be perfect; remember that you're not perfect either, because you both are only human.

> **Ask God to reveal any unrealistic expectations you may have for your marriage and change your expectations accordingly.**

Offer your wife patience, forgiveness, and unconditional love. Ask God to reveal any unrealistic expectations you may have for your marriage and change your expectations accordingly. Think and pray about what your purpose as a couple is in life, and once you've clarified that, seek to fulfill that purpose as you make daily decisions.

Recognize that living with purpose is more important than the irritations of daily life. Openly and honestly address and resolve misunderstandings with your wife, sharing your feelings with her, talking through offenses, and dealing with doubts you may have about her integrity, so you can build a truly trusting relationship.

RELATED SCRIPTURES
James 4:11

Don't speak evil against each other, my dear brothers and sisters. If you criticize each other and condemn each other, then you are criticizing and condemning God's law. But you are not a judge who can decide whether the law is right or wrong. Your job is to obey it.

Seek to avoid criticizing your wife. If there should come a time when constructive criticism is absolutely necessary, please be careful to do it with a lot of tender love and care.

Timing is everything. Wait until you are both in a good mood, and then ask her to sit with you. First tell her how much you love her and need her. Then tell her you need her help and then tell her what's on your mind. For example, after you have expressed your love to her, then say, "Sweetheart, I really love your cooking but, it could do with just a little less salt."

You do not want to be found fighting against God's law of "loving one another."

IF YOU REJECT THE ABOVE,
YOU WILL BE CREATING
THESE NEGATIVE CONSEQUENCES:

·   She feels like she's being counseled.
·   She feels unaccepted by you.
·   She has a loss of self-respect.
·   She develops a materialistic focus.

Believe me it is better to learn how to deal with the problems of your wife rather than trying to counsel her.

Notes

Chapter Four

THE TIME FACTOR

YOU MUST GIVE YOUR WIFE
ENOUGH TIME TO EXPRESS HERSELF
(HER IDEAS).

Most of the time, it will take a woman longer to express her ideas than for a man. You must patiently listen to your wife when she is speaking to you. First, because it may be just the idea you need. Secondly, your failure to do so will produce, in her, frustration and disillusionment. Therefore, we must relax, look her in the face and listen.

Husbands should understand that since women tend to be relationally oriented, words are very important to them. And we ought to learn from our helpmates because there is an old saying that goes: "Reliable communication permits progress."

Women are skilled at using words; in fact they learn to talk sooner than men do. There was a study done in which they rigged special microphones to record the noises that come out the mouths of little girls and boys. They found that 100% of the noises coming out of the mouths of little girls had something to do with conversation. They were either conversing with somebody else or conversing with someone imaginary or conversing with themselves. All of the noises that little girls (ages 2-4) were making had to do with conversation.

For little boys, it was discovered that only 60% of the sounds coming out of their mouths had to do with conversation. The other 40% were simply noises of animals or machines. So, the truth of the matter is that men start off behind women in talking and we never catch up. Little girls have a better

> **Women talk to express emotions... men talk to solve problems.**

ability to converse and communicate than little boys and this becomes a lifelong habit. As a result, women seem to understand the importance of clear communication better than men.

This is why women who hardly know each other can have a long and meaningful conversation. Perhaps you've heard of the husband who said, "Just the other night my wife was on the phone for nearly 30 minutes. When she hung up, I asked her 'Who was that?'"

She said, "Wrong number!"

Communication is one of the greatest sources of difficulty between men and women. Women talk to express emotions...men talk to solve problems. Whereas men tend to connect by doing things…women tend to connect with words.

Listen to the following conversation between a husband and wife and you'll see what I mean. A wife comes home from work and says, "I hate my job!"

The loving husband responds by saying, "Well, why don't you quit then?"

"No," she says, "it's just that there's so much work to do and not enough people."

The husband says, "Well, then tell your boss to hire some help for you."

She retorts, "Oh, why can't you ever just listen to me?"

And he, genuinely confused says, "I am listening to you. If you didn't want my advice, why did you bring up the subject?"

You see the man was focused on doing something. The wife was focused on relationship and on being heard. One wife expressed this to me once, "I want to be heard, not necessarily have my problems solved."

She said this because women have unique

RELATIONAL NEEDS...they need to know that their husbands are as committed to their relationship as they are. And just trying to fix everything will not do it.

RELATED SCRIPTURE
1 Corinthians 13:4
This love of which I speak is slow to lose patience, it looks for a way to being constructive.

To avoid making this awful blunder, love your wife with God's unmerited, unconditional and unlimited love. God's love for us is unmerited (we don't deserve it and can't earn it) – unconditional (it is not based on what we do or don't do) – and unlimited (it will never "run out" or be detained). You must accept and love your wife the same way.

IF YOU REJECT THE ABOVE
YOU WILL CREATE
THESE NEGATIVE CONSEQUENCES:

- She will envy you – want to be like you.
- She will try to express ideas like you, etc. but cannot.
- She will, with time, become very resentful toward you.
- She will not feel at ease when talking to you.

· She will let everything build up within and then try to unload all of it; just pour her heart out, all in one long sitting.

· She will clam up (stop talking) to you, to avoid being disappointed over and over again.

You must give her the time she needs to express herself and listen with patience or pay an awful price.

Chapter Five

THE PERFECT COMPLIMENT

YOU MUST PROJECT THE IDEA
THAT AS A TOTAL PERSON
YOUR WIFE IS THE PERFECT
COMPLEMENT TO YOU.

There is tendency, when the husband rejects his wife, to compare her appearance and abilities with women who process qualities she is lacking.

To avoid making this mistake, let me say this again, love your wife with God's unmerited, unconditional and unlimited love. God's love for us is unmerited (we don't deserve it and can't earn it), unconditional (it is not based on what we do or don't do), and unlimited (it will never "run out" or be detained).

You should accept and love your wife in like manner. Not only must we love our wives unconditionally, we must also learn to express unconditional love to our wives.

Now let's consider some ways to express unconditional love, so we can make our marriage better and satisfy our wives need to feel unconditional love.

Some women feel loved when their husbands show them affection. These people hear and receive affection best from a steady diet of encouraging words and sincere compliments.

The SONG OF SOLOMON, which is an ancient text about marital love, is written in this "love language." Throughout its pages the writer verbally expresses his love for his wife...complimenting her again and again. Listen to this excerpt:

> **There are some husbands who need to learn to express love like Solomon did when he spoke these words to his wife.** *"You are all beautiful my darling, there is no flaw in you."*

> *Your hair is like a flock of goats...your teeth are like freshly shorn sheep...your neck is like an ivory tower...your nose is like the tower of Lebanon.*

Now, I don't expect you men to be as good at this as King Solomon but you can try. I would however advise that you not compare your wife's nose to one of the largest towers in the mid-east. For some reason that worked back then but I don't think it would go over very well these days. But the point here is that for some affirming words is all it takes.

There are some husbands who need to learn to express love like Solomon did when he spoke these words to his wife. *"You are all beautiful my darling, there is no flaw in you."*

Some women feel loved when their husbands simply take the time to meaningfully interact with them, giving quality time. Quality time means giving someone your undivided attention...sitting on the couch with the TV off, looking at each other and talking for 20 minutes or more, etc. All husbands and wives need this kind of quality time together.

It has been said that in a typical week, the average married couple spends a total of a mere 37 minutes of time together. That's less than one-half of one percent of your time. Not much love can be shared in those brief moments. So some women only hear 'I love you' when their husbands give them meaningful things, not big things but meaningful things.

People who communicate love in this way feel unconditional love when spouses give them something that they can hold in their hands and says, "he was thinking of me," like a bottle of her favorite perfume or a beautiful piece of jewelry.

Some women hear 'I love you' best when their husbands do things for them. Like mopping the floor and taking out the trash without being asked, or maybe taking her car and having it cleaned up and filled with gas.

Now the list just goes on and on. Take the time to make a list of things you can say and do for your wife to express your love for her. Keep in mind you must act without being asked.

RELATED SCRIPTURES
Proverbs 31:28b – 29 [28b]
Her husband praises her; "There are many virtuous and capable women in the world, but you surpass them all!"

IF YOU REJECT THE ABOVE,
YOU WILL CREATE
THESE NEGATIVE CONSEQUENCES:
· She compares herself with other women.
· She hurts inwardly because of your remarks about other women.
· She fears that you will give someone else the attention she needs.
· She feels inadequate.

Notes

Chapter Six

WHAT IS IMPORTANT

YOU MUST SPEND ENOUGH TIME WITH YOUR WIFE TO KNOW WHAT IS IMPORTANT TO HER. LEARN TO LOOK AT LIFE FROM HER POINT OF VIEW.

Since we are often careless in seeing life from our wife's point of view, we often overlook or are insensitive to her care for certain details and the little extras she does in expressing her love.

You must maintain a high-level of sensitivity toward those certain details and little extras and express your approval. Because without this, your wife may become "weary in well doing."

HOW TO BE SENSITIVE WITH YOUR WIFE

Let's face it guys, most of you don't have a clue how to be sensitive! Well…let me clue you in on a few things… Here's what the dictionary says about it. Sensitivity, or being sensitive, is responsiveness to things around you. It's a general sense of what's going on.

But let's get a little more specific where your marriage is concerned. Don't think it's just a matter of self-awareness and a general idea of the world around you. The sensitivity your wife wants from you goes a little further. She's looking for a specific kind of sensitivity.

So what is this "specific kind of sensitivity" and how do you show her that you've got it? First off, don't be afraid to let her

> **Think about what it would be like if you were in her position.**

know how much you care. Express that she and her feelings are important to you. (She is important to you, right?????)

Second, you better make sure she knows her opinion is important to you. How do you do that? Open your mouth and tell her. Try listening for once to what she has to say. Then show her by your actions (more on that in a moment).

Third, put yourself in her place. Think about what it would be like if you were in her position.

Now, about putting all of this into action...Let's say my wife and I went out for an evening on the town and she forgot her jacket. I remembered my jacket. It's starting to get chilly. If I automatically give her my coat or offer it to her, this shows that I'm thinking of her first despite my own need for the coat.

Here's another example: you come home from work

and discover that your wife has had a really bad day and just needs a break. You have had a bad day as well but you tell her to sit down and put her feet up.

Now...you either fix dinner yourself, or you call and order dinner. To top it off you could even get the kids bathe and put them to bed. That's TRUE sensitivity for your wife, and I can guarantee you she will notice and that will be one of the best things you could do for her.

What matters here is that you are aware of your wife's needs, and you DO something about it. You can't just talk about it. You have to DO something about it.

How to take more interest in your wife's interests
Your wife is a busy woman. After she gets done with everything she has to do, she somehow finds time to do things she wants to do. And you want her to have that time for what she wants, but you also want some time to spend with her.

You don't understand her interests and you aren't sure if you want to. But if you gave her a chance to show you, you may discover that there is a lot more to your wife than you ever knew.

Start by asking your wife about her interests. Let her

talk as long as she wants to about them. Be an active part of the conversation, ask questions and verify what she says to make sure you understand. Talking will help you grow closer together and find new understanding.

> **If her interests aren't manly enough or challenging enough for you, don't just brush them off.**

After you have talked, take time to find out about her interests on your own. Be a good student. Do some research and find out new things that you can share with your wife next time you talk to her about her interests. This initiative will show her that you really care about her interests.

Try asking your wife if she can teach you. This can show her that you really want to learn, and that you feel she is intelligent. Give her a chance to share her knowledge and her feelings about her interests.

Keep an open mind. If her interests aren't manly enough or challenging enough for you, don't just brush them off. There could be more to them than you think. Make sure you give her all of the attention she deserves. If it is really important to you to spend time with your wife, then nothing should be too trivial.

Don't criticize your wife about her interests. Make

sure that you aren't making her feel bad about what she enjoys. If you are truly taking an interest in her, then don't make her think or feel that you are doing this out of obligation. In other words, be a willing participant.

When you are talking to your wife, listen carefully for clues of things that she wants to do, but hasn't. This may anything from a hobby to traveling. Take this knowledge and find a way to fulfill this dream with her. You can find many things in common when you venture into something that is new to both of you.

If your wife doesn't really feel like she wants to share all of her interests with you that is alright. Work together to find a new interest you can share. This may be taking a class together or learning a new skill together. This gives you common interests and time for yourself with different interests.

Make sure that you are becoming interested for the right reasons. Your intent should always be to show your wife love and interest. If you are expecting something in return then you don't have the right interest. Do it for her, not for what you can get out of it.

Spending time together is a very important aspect of

sharing but spending quality time is the best way to be. Doing something productive together can bring you closer together than you ever were.

Start spending time together like you did when you were courting. Learn something new about your wife and become excited all over again. Show interest in your wife and your marriage will benefit immensely. Don't forget to tell her you love her too.

RELATED SCRIPTURES
Philippians 2:4
Each of you should look not only to your own interests, but also to the interests of others.

1 Corinthians 10:24
Let no one seek his own, but each one the other's well-being.

1 Corinthians 13:4-5
Love suffers long and is kind; love does not envy; love does not parade itself, is not puffed up; does not behave rudely, does not seek its own, is not provoked, thinks no evil.

IF YOU REJECT THE ABOVE,
YOU WILL CREATE
THESE NEGATIVE CONSEQUENCES:

- She feels that she is not important to you.
- She feels lonely, even when she is with other people.
- She feels that your goals are going in the opposite direction.
- She feels insecure in her duties as a wife.

Please understand spending time with your wife is a very important matter. Also keep in mind this should be time without distractions so that both of you can talk openly with one another.

Chapter Seven

JUST SAY "NO"

YOU MUST DEVELOP THE CONFIDENCE TO SAY, "NO," WHEN PEOPLE SEEK TO PRESSURE YOU INTO ACTIVITIES AND RESPONSIBILITIES THAT TAKE AWAY FROM YOUR LEGITIMATE FAMILY TIME.

When your priorities are out of line, you will be pressured by secondary issues rather than the primary responsibilities God has given you for your wife and children.

Spend time with your wife. There is no substitute for spending time with her. She will be especially blessed when she thinks about the fact that you scheduled a block of time just to spend with her.

Whenever possible, enter into her world. Go where she is. When she has a recital, concert, game, program or awards ceremony, whatever the occasion, be there. This always requires the sacrifice of leaving your world – your agenda, priorities and comfort zone.

You must always do the same for your children. You must make free time for your family. Listen to the testimony of a man that I shall call, Mr. X.

"I'm a happily married man and a father of six children, and many readers ask me my secret to maintaining a happy marriage and a good relationship with my children.

> "My wife was as understanding as possible, but it was definitely a strain on our marriage when I seldom had time for her and the children."

"Well, there's no one secret, but a huge key for me has been; finding time to spend with them on a regular basis. That might sound obvious, but it's a problem for many couples and families.

"I know, because it was a problem for me not long ago – I was in a highly demanding and stressful job, and it often meant working late hours when my family wanted me to be home.

"My wife was as understanding as possible, but it was definitely a strain on our marriage when I seldom had time for her and the children. It was hard on the kids, as I would often miss their soccer games, school functions, and the like.

"It was hard on me too. I hated missing out on my family, and missed my wife and kids. So I made some changes in my life, simplifying, so that I could find the time I wanted to spend with my family.

"And I have to say, it's one of the smartest moves I've ever made. My wife and I have a stronger relationship than ever. My bond with my children is stronger than ever too, and I personally am happier than I've ever been."

But how do you free up time when you are busy and overworked?   Let me share with you some time-saving ideas

1.   Figure out what's essential.

What's most essential in your life? Make a long list of all the commitments in your life. Include   all the things you want to do. Then pick just 4-5. It can be difficult, but making these hard choices is crucial. My short list includes: spending time with family, writing, reading and running.

2.   Get out of commitments.

If a commitment doesn't line up with your short list of essentials, do all you can to get out of it. Sometimes that will mean disappointing people. That's OK. Your family is worth it.

3.   Simplify your schedule.

Other than commitments, are there other things you can get rid of on your schedule and to-do-list? Can you stop trying to do everything, and make time in your schedule? Don't pack your day full of appointments and tasks and projects. Leave space for your family.

4. Make dates.

Now that you've made some space in your life, make a standing appointment to spend time with your family. That might mean 20 minutes every evening when you come home with your wife, or a weekly date when you take her out. It may mean taking a walk or reading with your children every night, or a weekly 1-2 hour date with each child. Put it on the schedule, and make it the most sacred appointment you have.

5. Get the important stuff done early.

Figure out what is really important each morning, and do those things first. Otherwise, they get pushed back further and further and either don't get done, or make it necessary to work late.

6. Batch the small stuff.

Instead of interrupting the important tasks by doing small things like checking email, answering phones, or doing paperwork, do them in batches later in the day.

7.   Realize you won't get everything done. A to-do-list is unending. It will never get done. An email inbox is also never empty for long. So realize that there will always be more things to do, and decide you're OK with that. Don't try to get everything done.

8.   Do less.
Along the same lines, focus on doing less and less. This will mean you're going to focus on doing the important things, and cut down on the less important things. When you've cut down on the number of things you're doing, try to cut some more. Less is better.

9.   Cut back on meetings.
Think about the last 4 or 5 meetings to which you've gone. How many of them were really valuable? How many of them did you need to attend? It depends on your job, but sometimes you can beg out of a meeting (or just outright cancel it if you have that power) and accomplish the same results through an email or two. You just saved yourself 30 to 60 minutes per meeting canceled.

10.   Watch less TV.
Many people watch hours of TV a day. You can easily save an hour a day if you cut some TV, just watch your single favorite show each day. Don't channel

surf.

11.   Limit your time online.
If you're like me, you can spend hours a day reading online. Limit your online reading and focus on your essential tasks.

12.   Start work early.
If possible, start your work-day at an earlier hour, before everyone else does. You won't have constant interruptions and distractions. You'll be amazed how much you can get done between 6am and 8am. Much more can be accomplished with shorter breaks and lunch hours. Then, perhaps, you can be home at an earlier hour with the family.

13.   Say no.
One of the biggest groups of time eaters is requests from other people. All day long we get requests in person, on the phone, in emails, through paperwork, for meetings, for assignments, for information, to be on a committee or team; these are all requests that will eat up your time. Say no to all but the essentials.

14.   Stop checking email.
This doesn't work for everyone, but if you can stop checking email except at one or two times during the day, you can free up a lot of wasted time. Checking

email constantly takes up a lot of time.

15.   Remember your priority.
When making choices, or saying yes to others'
demand on your time, remember what's really
important to you -- your wife, and your family, not
other people's needs. Always keep that in mind.

Now let me mention one other thing.   Most men
wouldn't think of doing such a thing, and there was a
time in my life when I wouldn't have either.

When God changed me, He showed me that my time
is not my own. He gave it to me, and He wants me to
bless my wife by giving "more" time to her.

God makes time for us. If you really want to be like
Him, make her need for time with you a priority in
your life.

Practical Ways to Give Your Wife Time:

- Time to pray together every day
- Time to study the Word together
- Time to go to church and sit together and later talk about what you heard together
- Time to go walking together when you won't be interrupted
- Time to go for drives to places you both like — the woods, the hills, the mountains, or the beach
- Time to go to bed together and talk without being distracted by the television
- Time to help with grocery shopping and carrying in the groceries
- Time to go out for dinner with her when you were planning to watch the Super Bowl (That's a great way to beat the crowds at your favorite restaurant!)
- Time to open doors for her
- Time to help her put on her coat
- Time to make breakfast for her and the children on weekends

RELATED SCRIPTURES:
Ephesians 5:16
.... making the most of every opportunity, because the days are evil.

Psalm 90:12
Teach us to number our days aright, that we may gain a heart of wisdom.

IF YOU REJECT THE ABOVE,
YOU WILL CREATE THESE
NEGATIVE CONSEQUENCES:

· She will lose respect for you.

· She will resent you and whoever is infringing upon her time with you.

· She will doubt that your true love is for her.

· She will develop inner resentment for your vocation and outside activities.

· She feels you don't practice what you preach.

You must spend quality time with your wife and children because it is too expensive to neglect. A sensitive husband/father perceives the needs of his wife and children and does what he must to meet them. Sensitivity toward your wife will open doors of communication and intimacy you never thought possible.

Chapter Eight

DISCIPLINE YOUR CHILDREN

YOU MUST DETERMINE THE GOALS AND THE GUIDELINES FOR DISCIPLINING YOUR CHILDREN.

The husband not only has the responsibility to establish the goals and guidelines for discipline, but he must take full responsibility for it. When he fails to do so, it puts added responsibilities on an already over worked wife. This will also result in the children playing one parent against the other.

Biblical discipline must be based on love. It is hard work because it is a balancing act between punishment and biblical discipline.

Let's look first of all at the matter of "biblical discipline." We must first and foremost seek to cultivate righteousness in children's hearts.

Paul says in Ephesians 6:4, *"And you, fathers, do not provoke your children to wrath, but bring them up in the training and admonition of the Lord."*

Hebrews 12:11 also says, *"Now no chastening seems to be joyful for the present, but painful; nevertheless, afterward it yields the peaceable fruit of righteousness to those who have been trained by it."*

Our first concern must be to cultivate righteousness in the heart. Let's look now at, "biblical punishment."

Regardless of how well informed parents may consider themselves, their children's attitudes constantly test their disciplinary techniques.

Proverbs 13:24a says, *"He who spares his rod hates his son."*

This verse must be taken with Ephesians 6:4. Yes, there comes a time when a father must dish out punishment, but you must not let it get out of hand.

How then should a Christian father discipline his children? Regardless of how well informed parents may consider themselves, their children's attitudes constantly test their disciplinary techniques. When a child misbehaves, parents review their disciplinary strategies: frowns, reprimands, the trusty removal of a valued toy or activity, etc.

Parents tend to sigh in relief when they find an efficient formula for discipline. By using that now-proven method, they can anticipate a satisfactory response each time. In the process, however, the focus may shift away from considering God's role in the discipline process.

Christian parents desire God to work through them *"for it is God who works in you to will and to act according to his good purpose"* (Philippians 2:13).

Christians administer discipline by allowing God to be their starting point rather than an afterthought. What is the starting point when determining "how should a Christian discipline children?"

Parents must first examine their own character. Children learn by example and by observing Godly attitudes in their parents' lives. Consistency is the first step towards successful results. If a child is reluctant to perform their chores, they may not comprehend the concept of servant hood in their family.

Is serving taught in a home where the father defers all household chores to the mother? Or is rudeness or disrespect modeled in a mother's phone conversations and "innocent" gossip?

The purpose of any discipline is to leave an impression. The purpose of Christian discipline is to leave an eternal impression. *"I have set you an example that you should do as I have done for you. I tell you the truth, no servant is greater than his master, nor is a messenger greater than the one who sent him "* (John 13:15-16).

Imagine Jesus modeling service, humility and obedience with one gesture! Christian discipline is not sporadic, depending on convenience or circumstances. Whether in public, at grandma's or at home, the process should be consistent.

> **The discipline process requires significant time and commitment.**

Correction and instruction will then be opportunities for God to work through parents in any situation. Consequently, the discipline process requires significant time and commitment.

How should a Christian discipline children using forgiveness? Poor discipline manipulates a child by using cruel words and threats. For example, the thermometer is reading 100 degrees outside and the air conditioner has ceased to function. The dog just wiggled under the fence and your wife is sick with the flu. Little Susie whines, "I'm hot! I want a Popsicle!" for the tenth time.

You finally snap, "I'm hot too and sick and tired of your whining! Now shut up and go to your room!"

Minutes later you begin to calm down and feel miserable and guilty. Fortunately, there is a right response to a parent's wrong behavior. Susie needs to hear that she deserved correction, but not a cruel response.

Christian parents are not perfect! We make mistakes. The difference Christ makes is in giving us grace and His example of forgiveness. By taking the time to apologize and reaffirm her love, Susie's father is softening his own heart as well as his daughter's.

Then both father and child can take the opportunity to pray for forgiveness and for God's Spirit to guide them in the future. Our children respect us when we are honest with them. Our children learn to respect God because He is always truthful with them.

"But when he, the Spirit of truth, comes, he will guide you into all truth…" (John 16:13).

How should a Christian discipline children using spiritual guidance? As you set goals for Christian discipline, there are three key questions you can ask:
·   Why is biblical discipline important to the Lord?
·   Why does He require you to do specific things or to take certain actions as a parent?
·   How does the lesson I am teaching coincide with the Lord's plan for my child?

Christians use discipline to encourage their child's spiritual nature, not the child's natural instincts. Learn as many ways of responding to your child as you can, while always speaking and acting in love.

Then, as children mature, they will reflect the character of Jesus Christ. "And Jesus grew in wisdom and stature, and in favor with God and men."

RELATED SCRIPTURES:
Hebrews 12:10-13
For they indeed for a few days chastened us as seemed best to them, but He for our profit, that we may be partakers of His holiness. Now no chastening seems to be joyful for the present, but painful; nevertheless, afterward it yields the peaceable fruit of righteousness to those who have been trained by it. Therefore strengthen the hands which hang down, and the feeble knees, and make straight paths for your feet, so that what is lame may not be dislocated, but rather be healed.

Ephesians 6:4
And you, fathers, do not provoke your children to wrath, but bring them up in the training and admonition of the Lord.

Proverbs 13:24
*He who spares his rod hates his son, but he who loves
him disciplines him promptly.*

Malachi 4:5-6
*Behold, I will send you Elijah the prophet, before the
coming of the great and dreadful day of the Lord.
And he will turn the hearts of the fathers to the
children, and the hearts of the children to their
fathers, Lest I come and strike the earth with a
curse. "*

IF YOU REJECT THE ABOVE, YOU WILL CREATE THESE NEGATIVE CONSEQUENCES:

· She feels rejected by the children
· She resents you for not assuming your responsibilities
· She feels that you degrade her in front of the children
· She lacks confidence in your authority and responsibility

If you do not determine the goals and the guidelines
for the disciplining of your children, you do your wife
and your children a gross injustice.

Chapter Nine

THE POWER OF TIME

YOU MUST PROVIDE
FOR YOUR WIFE
ADEQUATE TIME TO DISCUSS
THE NECESSARY PREPARATION
FOR MAJOR CHANGES.

Your wife will be able to make major adjustments if you have taken the time to explain the reasons behind the action and have given adequate time to make the change. Inadequate time will cause her to become insecure and apprehensive.

Therefore, you should take the time to thoroughly explain exactly the type of change you wish to make. After you explain, then give the reason or reasons you want to make the change.

Then explain to her what result you expect if the change is made and what you expect will happen if the change is not made. After that, let your wife know that she has time to think and pray about it and that you will be praying for her. Better yet, let her hear you praying for her.

This might also be a good time to remember that a woman's intuitiveness is oftentimes more accurate than a man's logic. This is clearly emphasized by her greater emotional sensitivity to the needs of the children.

Failure to give her enough time to make changes and express what she feels my produce frustration and feeling of inadequacy within her .

RELATED SCRIPTURES:
Proverbs 3:5-6
Trust in the Lord with all your heart, And lean not on your own understanding; In all your ways acknowledge Him, And He shall direct your paths.

Proverbs 11:14
Where there is no counsel, the people fall; but in the multitude of counselors there is safety.

Proverbs 19:20
Listen to counsel and receive instruction, that you may be wise in your latter days.

IF YOU FAIL TO DO THE ABOVE, YOU WILL CREATE THESE NEGATIVE CONSEQUENCES:

- She feels emotionally drained.
- She becomes apprehensive.
- She feels you are inconsiderate and indifferent toward her, and the family.
- She feels she is not important.

You must provide the necessary time for your wife to make preparation for major changes.

Chapter Ten

DISCIPLINE

YOU MUST BECOME DISCIPLINED IN YOUR INWARD ATTITUDES AND OUTWARD ACTIONS TOWARD YOUR WIFE.

A wife is very sensitive about honesty and moral purity in her husband.

ABOUT HONESTY
In a mature relationship, honesty is the best policy. It may be difficult, but the truth will allow relationships to breathe. No matter what happens, no one can ever challenge the fact that you are truthful, which might mean that the other person also gives you the same respect.

If something doesn't suit you let them know. Otherwise they will not trust your opinion. But make it sound like a compliment. Suggest an alternative, and attach praise to the alternative. For example, if she ask you if you like an article of clothing she is trying on (trying on, not already wearing at a party) let her know that it might work, but you think the blue one is your favorite so far because it shows off her great (insert a feature you appreciate, preferably not one that she is self-conscious about).

It's not going to be easy to be honest and kind at the

same time, so focus on learning how to give a feedback sandwich and you'll both be better off.

> Even if we individually take moral purity seriously, we are surrounded by media and culture that celebrate sex as the currency of the realm.

ABOUT PURITY

In today's world sexual immorality is playing Russian roulette. It puts the lives of you and your wife at risk. There is the problem of venereal diseases, AIDS, Herpes and the experts are telling us that the dreaded Syphilis is back along with some unnamed stuff. There has never been a better time to exercise self-control. Your wife's admiration for you is greatly diminished when you exercise a lack of self-control.

We live in a time of great moral pollution. Even if we individually take moral purity seriously, we are surrounded by media and culture that celebrate sex as the currency of the realm. Immodesty commands our attention. Lust encourages our warped thinking. Our screen heroes and our real life national heroes are as casual about sex as about a night on the town. Our contemporary attitude toward sex creates a desolating scourge.

Spencer W. Kimball, in his book, <u>The Miracle of</u>

<u>Forgiveness</u> (pg. 250), warned us that "infidelity is one of the great sins of our generation. The movies, the books, the magazine stories all seem to glamorize the faithlessness of husbands and wives.

To the world nothing is holy, not even marriage vows...It reminds us of Isaiah, who said: *"Woe unto them that call evil good and good evil..."* (Isaiah 5:20).

ABOUT OUR EXAMPLE
One of the great examples of moral ascendance was Joseph of Israel. His encounter with Potiphar's wife is told in just six verses in the book of Genesis.

And it came to pass after these things, that his master's wife cast her eyes upon Joseph and she said, "Lie with me." But he refused, and said unto his master's wife, "Look, my master does not know what is with me in the house, and he has committed all that he hath to my hand. There is none greater in this house than I, neither hath he kept back anything from me but you, because you are his wife. How then can I do this great wickedness, and sin against God?"

And it came to pass, as she spoke to Joseph day by day, that he did not heed her, to lie by her, or to be with her. But it happened about this time when Joseph went into the house to do his work and none of the men of the house was inside. And she caught him by his garment, saying, "Lie with me" and he left his garment in her hand, and fled, and ran outside. (Genesis 39:7-12)

We honor Joseph's valiance and purity. He was far from his homeland with its attendant accountability. Potiphar's wife was alluring and powerful. Yet he resisted her without hesitation. What an example!

RELATED SCRIPTURES:
1 Thessalonians 4:3-5
For this is the will of God, your sanctification: that you should abstain from sexual immorality; that each of you should know how to possess his own vessel in sanctification and honor, not in passion of lust, like the Gentiles who do not know God.

1 Corinthians 6:18-20
Flee sexual immorality. Every sin that a man does is outside the body, but he who commits sexual immorality sins against his own body. Or do you not know that your body is the temple of the Holy Spirit who is in you, whom you have from God, and you are not your own? For you were bought at a price;

therefore glorify God in your body and in your spirit, which are God's.

Ephesians 5:3
But fornication and all uncleanness or covetousness, let it not even be named among you, as is fitting for saints.

Colossians 3:5
Therefore put to death your members which are on the earth: fornication, uncleanness, passion, evil desire, and covetousness, which is idolatry.

IF YOU REJECT THE ABOVE, YOU CREATE THE FOLLOWING NEGATIVE CONSEQUENCES:

·   She loses her admiration for you.

·   She becomes cold and indifferent to your physical needs.

·   She develops an "I don't care" attitude.

In your attitudes and actions toward your wife you must maintain a high level of sensitivity toward her.

Chapter Eleven

SPIRITUAL LEADERSHIP

THERE MUST BE
A CONTINUAL DEVELOPMENT
OF SPIRITUAL LEADERSHIP
BY YOU, THE HUSBAND.

You must provide spiritual stability for your wife. When you fail to do this or show disinterest, the long-range results will be severe for your children and place unnecessary burdens on your wife.

Most men desire to be good husbands but are not always sure what that looks like. Of course, the best place to begin is simply to ask your wife for her input!

Alongside of this, however, there are many practical things that husbands can keep in mind. A good husband thrives on being a "shock absorber" for his wife by anticipating his wife's needs and fears.

Here are three practical ways
to provide leadership for you wife.

First, encourage self-worth. The factors that affect feelings of self-worth are usually obvious: intellect, appearance, productivity, success in relationships and financial freedom, among others. Discover mutual areas of interest with your wife and work at communications in that area.

Some of the best ways to encourage your wife include, seeking out her intellectual interests and finding one where she can teach you. Show interest in her appearance, and support her desire to have a sufficient wardrobe for career and social events.

> **Become an expert on her abilities. If she has a hobby, encourage her.**

Become an expert on her abilities. If she has a hobby, encourage her. Look for ways to involve her talents publicly. If she is a mother, help her develop in-home income, if she desires it. Assist with household chores and especially be involved in raising your children.

Be aware of her relationships and assist her in developing friends. Help her organize her schedule. Steps like these help to build her self-worth.

Second, provide comfort. Never allow your wife to experience pain without sharing it with her. A death in the family, a difficult child, frustration in her career, or a disappointment in relationships may require your help. Comfort her and take responsibility for helping her find a solution.

Third, facilitate spiritual maturity. Your hope for mutual faith in your marriage is related to your wife's maturity as well as yours. Do everything possible to assist her spiritual interest. Encourage her efforts to minister to others or attend church functions. As a couple get involved in small groups or Sunday school.

One of her greatest joys, however, will be watching you take spiritual leadership in your home and church. Many wives have expressed their joy in seeing their husbands excel spiritually.

When a husband does not supply leadership, women take the leadership because women are concerned about the welfare of the family.

Leadership must be done in love. If a man demands submission, a woman will not give it willingly. Therefore love must first come from the man. Women are responders and will respond to love by willingly submitting to the authority of leadership. Submission is not a right to be demanded, but it is a divine responsibility to be fulfilled. The husband is responsible for setting the spiritual priorities in the home regarding the family's relationship to church and to God.

Joshua 24:15 says,

> *And if it seems evil to you to serve the Lord, choose for yourselves this day whom you will serve, whether the gods which your fathers*

served that were on the other side of the River, or the gods of the Amorites, in whose land you dwell. But as for me and my house, we will serve the Lord.

> **You cannot provide spiritual leadership for her until she knows that you really love the Lord.**

I believe the best way to accomplish this is to model for her.

Deuteronomy 6:5 says, *"You shall love the Lord your God with all your heart, with all your soul, and with all your strength."*

Does your wife know that you truly love the Lord? You cannot provide spiritual leadership for her until she knows that you really love the Lord. I also believe you must model Proverbs 3:5-6 for her:

> *Trust in the Lord with all your heart, and lean not on your own understanding; In all your ways acknowledge Him, And He shall direct your paths.*

When your wife knows that you love and trust God, then she will be able to surrender to you as her spiritual leader.

RELATED SCRIPTURES
Exodus 20:3-5

You shall have no other gods before Me. You shall not make for yourself a carved image, or any likeness of anything that is in heaven above, or that is in the earth beneath, or that is in the water under the earth; you shall not bow down to them nor serve them. For I, the Lord your God, am a jealous God, visiting the iniquity of the fathers on the children to the third and fourth generations of those who hate Me

1 Timothy 5:8

But if anyone does not provide for his own, and especially for those of his household, he has denied the faith and is worse than an unbeliever.

1 Peter 3:7

Husbands, likewise, dwell with them with understanding, giving honor to the wife, as to the weaker vessel, and as being heirs together of the grace of life, that your prayers may not be hindered.

IF YOU FAIL TO DO THE ABOVE,
YOU WILL CREATE
THESE NEGATIVE CONSEQUENCES:

·   She will develop resentment for the burden of spiritual development of the family being placed on her.

·   She will look down on you as the leader of the home.

You are God's man in the home, therefore, you must tell the truth about God by what you say and what you do.

Notes

Chapter Twelve

WATCH YOUR MOUTH

YOU MUST AVOID
JOKING AND JESTING
AT YOUR WIFE'S EXPENSE
IN FRONT OF OTHERS.

There is a tendency for some husbands to joke and make cutting remarks about their wives in front of others. This is usually an attempt to get her to change some characteristic that he dislikes.

If you want to see change in your wife, joking about it in the presence of others will only make matters worst. Jokes are serious. The line between a friendly jibe and a humiliating stab is often a fine one. You have to question whether the laughter you may get is worth the pain you may inflict.

This is true regarding every humorous comment made about another person. But between husband and wife, humiliation is simply criminal. It goes against everything that a marriage is supposed to be, an exclusive oneness.

In the Jewish wedding ceremony, after standing under the *chuppah* (marriage canopy), the bride and groom are taken to a private room, known as the *yichud* room. *Yichud* means "oneness," "unity" and "exclusivity."

By entering this room, a secluded place where no one is present but the couple, they create a sacred space that is theirs and theirs alone. The newlyweds leave the *yichud* room after a few minutes, but in a way they should never leave it. The privacy and oneness of the *yichud* room should be taken with them in their marriage.

> The relationship between husband and wife is a sacred and secluded place, and should stay that way.

The relationship between husband and wife is a sacred and secluded place, and should stay that way. Any word or action that jeopardizes the privacy and unity of a marriage should be erased from our repertoire.

When you make fun of your wife in front of your friends, you have momentarily stepped out of the *yichud* room. You have abandoned your soul-partner, leaving her alone and isolated just for a few cheap laughs. To make a joke is fine, but never at the expense of your oneness.

The same thing happens when you criticize her in public. In doing so, you have allowed strangers into the yichud room. You have invited others into a moment that should only be between the two of you. There is a time and a place for criticism in a relationship, but not in the presence of others.

These mistakes are so common that, to many couples, they have become acceptable. But it's these little things that can erode a good marriage. For a relationship to thrive it must always remain an exclusive oneness. Once you get comfortable in the yichud room, you'll never want to leave.

You will get much better results by always speaking well of her in the presence of others. If you know about a weakness or a fault in the life of your wife, keep it in your own heart.

Proverbs 10:12 says, *"Hatred stirs up strife, but love covers all sins."*

Proverbs 31:28 says, *"Her children rise up and call her blessed; Her husband also, and he praises her."*

Look for a time and place when you can privately share with your wife that thing that troubles you. Pray and trust God to give you the power to accept your wife as she is.

RELATED SCRIPTURE:
Ephesians 5:4
....neither filthiness, nor foolish talking, nor coarse jesting, which are not fitting, but rather giving of thanks.

IF YOU REJECT THE ABOVE,
YOU WILL CREATE THE FOLLOWING
NEGATIVE CONSEQUENCES:

- She is injured in her spirit.
- She feels embarrassed around others.
- She has a fear of expressing her opinions.
- She becomes discouraged in developing positive qualities and then having them "shot down."

Always look for kind and flattering things to say to your wife both in public and in private. This will meet a great need in her life.

Notes

Chapter Thirteen

FORGIVE

YOU MUST FORGIVE
THE PAST FAILURES
OF YOUR WIFE.

Yes, be willing to completely forgive the wrongs done in the past. Do not develop an unforgiving attitude. An unforgiving attitude will cause your family to break-up.

I've been thinking what a strange and awful beast, the grudge. Acting like an internal contract, the grudge obligates us to be unhappy and unhealed. Sometimes a grudge starts with a tangible offense, but over time it imbeds itself cleverly. All that's left then is a sensation of mistrust or dislike. On the other hand, sometimes we remember the intricate details of our resentment. Grudges are fortresses of the malcontent.

I have found unforgiveness is an internal viewpoint hurting the wounded more than the wrongdoer. The offender may carry on with life whereas the injured person clutches to new pain with the memory of the transgression. Those negative memories and feelings bring repeated sufferings. Some wrongs seem unforgivable because they are unforgettable.

To me, it is a myth that forgiving equals forgetting. Forgiveness is purely the waiving of our right to penalize. Forgiving is forgetting that you should blame or punish the one who hurt you. Forgetting a wrong done to you may end up as wasted life experience.

> **Don't be fooled – forgiveness does not vindicate an offense. It is forgiveness that releases us from the offense.**

Don't be fooled – forgiveness does not vindicate an offense. It is forgiveness that releases us from the offense. A forgiver quits shouldering the burden of injustice, and receives in its place freedom and eventual healing. As we release the right to retaliate, blessings and opportunities flood into our lives because grudges are dams that hold back liberation.

My friend experienced many difficult years deprived of family love and support because resentment had blocked the way for everyone concerned. Once that dam was broken renewal began to flow, just as water in a parched land brings life and bounty.

Listen to what Paul says in Colossians 3:12-13

> *Therefore, as the elect of God, holy and beloved, put on tender mercies, kindness, humility, meekness, longsuffering; [13] bearing with one another, and forgiving one another, if anyone has a complaint against*

another; even as Christ forgave you, so you also must do.

Notice the phrase, "even as Christ forgave you, so you also must do." When we have been hurt, this doesn't come very easily.   Nevertheless, apart from real forgiveness, there is not much hope for a marriage.

Unforgiving attitudes are very destructive.   Decide ahead of time to forgive the future wounds and offenses of your wife.   Realize that failure to forgive reflects an attitude to, "get even" and a preoccupation with self-pity and pride.

Although it may not be easy, I encourage you to attain emancipation right away as you search for any unforgiveness in your heart and mind. Whether from the past or the present, cancel the debt owed you.

If possible, tell the perpetrator you have forgiven them, (without expecting anything in return.) If that is not feasible, in your own heart fully break the grudge dam with forgiveness and enjoy the coming freedom. Forgiveness is a gracious gift; allowing forgiveness to release and heal you is an immeasurable reward.

RELATED SCRIPTURES
Matthew 6:14-15

For if you forgive men their trespasses, your heavenly Father will also forgive you. But if you do not forgive men their trespasses, neither will your Father forgive your trespasses.

IF YOU REJECT THE ABOVE, YOU WILL CREATE THE FOLLOWING NEGATIVE CONSEQUENCES:

- She questions the sincerity of your love.
- She reacts to attitudes of superiority.
- She justifies her own negative attitudes and offenses toward you.

You may never forget a hurt, but you can forgive and put it behind you. You must forgive for your own peace of mind and good health.

Notes

Chapter Fourteen

HONESTY

YOU MUST BE HONEST
AND VERBALLY ADMIT
WHEN YOU ARE WRONG

You must recognize that communication with your wife is your responsibility and that honor and respect are the result of being willing to admit a wrong and ask forgiveness.

Listen to the words of Proverbs 19:5: *"A false witness will not go unpunished, And he who speaks lies will not escape."*

Listen to Proverbs 26:28 also: *"A lying tongue hates those who are crushed by it, And a flattering mouth works ruin."*

According to these scriptures honesty is definitely the best way to go. It is a wise man who confesses and renounces it, when he is wrong.

Proverbs 28:13 says, *"He who covers his sins will not prosper, But whoever confesses and forsakes them will have mercy."*

Let me suggest that before you confess something that could destroy your marriage, talk to your pastor or someone you know to be a mature Christian. If necessary, consult a Christian Professional Counselor.

However, you must keep this in mind: Honesty and trust are vital to a healthy marriage. This lesson offers insight to this critical aspect of any relationship. One of the major reasons for the breakdown in relationships is dishonesty and betrayal of trust.

Nothing causes more profound damage and hurt than betrayal in your relationship.

It has been said by wiser people than me, that without trust, there can be no love. Nothing causes more profound damage and hurt than betrayal in your relationship. Lying about money, feelings and other key issues can damage a marriage irreparably.

One of my counsel-ties is still suffering from the effects of these 15 years after her marriage ended. She had married someone she had known for several years, and believed absolutely he was marrying her for the same reason -- love.

Two years into the marriage, he told her one night he had never truly loved her, and had married her because it was "expected" of him. On top of this, he had systematically raided their joint accounts and left her with nothing. Because of this dishonesty, she has never remarried and has a hard time believing in her own self-worth.

In order for a relationship to succeed, truthfulness and trust need to be firmly established. If you don't want children or have doubts about your feelings, don't lie. It isn't fair. Chances are your wife senses these things anyway.

Don't use truth as a weapon to hurt your wife. Telling your wife she doesn't measure up to past partners is very, very harmful. Exposing a person's flaws in a cold and cutting manner is also cruel. Not one of us is perfect. Hurting someone this way is totally unnecessary.

Bringing up past partners is a guaranteed way to rupture a relationship. Don't mistake stupidity for honesty either. Telling your wife how many partners you've slept with isn't going to improve your sexual relationship one bit. Instead, you may find your spouse in silent competition with the "ghosts" occupying your bed.

If you have children you've given up for adoption or had taken away, be honest from the start. Don't wait until after you're married to spring this kind of unpleasant surprise.

If both of you have an agreement to wait to have children, don't plan an accidental pregnancy. This can cause years of resentment both towards you and the child.

> **Do some self analysis: Are there any major areas of dishonesty in your marriage?**

Past problems, including bankruptcy, jail, marriages gone wrong and illness need to be disclosed. In many states failure to do so can be cause for annulment. If you have incurred debts you are having trouble repaying, be truthful about it.

Enlist your wife's help in looking for solutions. Don't let a lack of honesty ruin your marriage. It's never too late in ANY marriage to start over.

Do some self analysis: Are there any major areas of dishonesty in your marriage?

Now let me ask you some more questions.

Do you think we (as Christians) should ALWAYS tell the truth, the whole truth and nothing but the truth?

Do you think we shouldn't ALWAYS tell the truth...?

Are you not holding up your hand because you're

sensing a trap here? Have you seen that Geico commercial on TV where the woman comes into the kitchen and asks her husband, "Do you think this dress makes me look fat?"

Do you remember what that husband said? "Yes, of course it does!"

All across America, you can hear the collective groan of men as they lift themselves out of easy chairs and shout: "NO! Don't say that!"

That man may have told his wife the truth... but that particular truth wasn't the smartest thing he ever said. I prefer the answer a man gave to his wife when she asked: "Do I look fat?"

To which he replied: "Do I look stupid?"

LOOK with me in Ephesians 4:29:
> *Let no corrupt communication proceed out of your mouth, but that which is good to the use of edifying, that it may minister grace unto the hearers.*

Now, what I'm going to say next may make you uncomfortable. It makes me uncomfortable. But I'm convinced this is a Biblical concept: The only time we shouldn't be telling the truth, the whole truth and nothing but the truth... is when that truth damages or destroys the people around us.

You might ask, "Blue, how can you say that?"

Well, I can say that because I believe it's Biblical. One of the most unusual stories in Scripture is told in the Exodus 1. There, we're told that the Egyptians began to fear the Israelites that lived in their country.

Then the Pharaoh gave an order to the Hebrew midwives who always helped women deliver their babies.

When you help the Hebrew women in childbirth and observe them on the delivery stool, if it is a boy, kill him; but if it is a girl, let her live."

The midwives, however, feared God and did not do what the king of Egypt had told them to do; they let the boys live. Then the king of Egypt summoned the midwives and asked them, "Why have you done this? Why have you let the boys live?"

The midwives answered Pharaoh, "Hebrew women are not like Egyptian women; they are vigorous and give birth before the midwives arrive." (Exodus

1:16-19)

Now, were the midwives honest? No... they lied! These women were speaking to the Hitler of their day, the Stalin of their era. He was a thug intent on murdering all the boy children in Israel. Had they told him the truth there is no telling what evil he would have devised...

BUT THEY LIED! Yes they lied... And what did God think of their action? Exodus 1:20-21 says,
> *So God was kind to the midwives and the people increased and became even more numerous. And because the midwives feared God, he gave them families of their own.*

He rewarded them! WHY? Because, what they did, they did for God. They didn't lie because they feared for their own lives. They lied because they "feared God."

My point is simply that: The only time we shouldn't be telling the truth, the whole truth and nothing but the truth... is when that truth damages or destroys the people around us.

I once knew a man who was "honest" with his wife. He told her what a bad housekeeper she was,

He told her what a rotten mother she was. He told her how unattractive she was. He emotionally browbeat her until she began to tell falsehoods to protect herself from his constant accusations. Then when he caught her telling lies...he told her that she was a liar.

> **This husband spoke "truth" to his wife. But it wasn't a "wholesome" truth.**

Now what he told her always had a measure of truth to it.

· She probably wasn't the best housekeeper in the world.

· She probably wasn't the perfect mother.

· She may not have won any beauty contests.

· And she did lie to avoid his emotional abuse.

This husband spoke "truth" to his wife. But it wasn't a "wholesome" truth. It was NOT a truth he used to "edify" her. It was truth intended to drag her down and destroy her.

Paul tells us: *"Do not let any unwholesome talk come out of your mouths, but only what is helpful for building others up according to their needs, that it may benefit those who listen."* (Ephesians 4:29)

We should always *"Be kind and compassionate to*

one another..." (Ephesians 4:32)

RELATED SCRIPTURE
James 5:16
Therefore confess your sins to each other and pray for each other so that you may be healed. The prayer of a righteous man is powerful and effective.

IF YOU REJECT THE ABOVE,
YOU WILL CREATE
THESE NEGATIVE CONSEQUENCES:

· She lacks humility toward you.
· She develops a wounded spirit.
· She develops coolness toward you.

Do not be afraid to be honest and admit it when you are wrong. Proverbs 19:5 tells us why: *"A false witness will not go unpunished, And he who tells lies will not escape."*

Chapter Fifteen

CLARIFICATION

YOU MUST DEFINE
AND CLARIFY
YOUR BASIC RESPONSIBILITIES
WITH YOUR WIFE.

It is essential that the husband communicate his frame of reference to his wife. This must be done by specifically identifying what you feel are your responsibilities. No matter what you feel your responsibilities are, you must make it very clear to your wife so the two of you can be on the same page.

It is also necessary for you to clarify which areas of your responsibilities you feel, overlap her responsibilities. It is absolutely critical that you and your wife develop a plan for working through those areas in which the responsibilities overlap.

With the advent of so many dual career marriages, the division of domestic responsibilities has become a major source of marital conflict. Changes in our cultural values have contributed greatly to the problem, because there is more agreement that both a husband and wife should share these responsibilities, particularly childcare. But change in behavior has not kept pace with the change in values.

Traditionally, wives have assumed most household and child care responsibilities, while husbands have taken the responsibility of providing income for the family. But today, at least in America men are changing the diapers, wielding the mop and tending the stove more often than ever before, it still isn't enough.

> In dual-career marriages, men on average don't do half as much childcare and housework as their working wives.

In dual-career marriages, men on average don't do half as much childcare and housework as their working wives. As most women have figured out by now, men are not very motivated to do childcare and housekeeping.

Domestic responsibilities are a time bomb in many marriages. Marriages usually begin with a willingness of both spouses to share domestic responsibilities. Newlyweds commonly wash dishes together, make the bed together, and divide many household tasks.

The groom welcomes the help he gets from his wife because, prior to marriage he'd been doing it all alone as a bachelor. At this point in marriage, neither of them regard domestic responsibilities as an important marital issue. But the time bomb is ticking.

When does it explode? It's when the children arrive! Children create huge needs, both a greater need for income and greater domestic responsibilities. The previous division of labor is now obsolete.

Both spouses must take on new responsibilities. Which ones should they take? In most modern marriages, both spouses opt for income, leaving the domestic responsibilities to whoever will volunteer.

It's a recipe for disaster, at least for most working women, because they end up doing most of the housework and childcare, while resenting their husbands' lack of support.

If household responsibilities are given to whoever is in the mood to do them, nothing much will be done. If one spouse demands help from the other, that will also have an unsatisfactory outcome. But if assignment of these tasks can be mutually agreed upon, by willing spouses that accept the responsibility, everything will run smoothly.

This solution will require you to do something that you may rarely do – get organized! It means you must think through your problem carefully and systematically. You will need to write down your objectives and create solutions that take each other's feelings into account.

You may find all of this awkward and terrible, but you must understand – there is no other way! Besides, when you're done, you may find it to be more comfortable than you anticipated.

NOW LET ME GIVE YOU
FOUR SUGGESTED STEPS:
Step 1: Identify your household responsibilities.
First, make a list of all your household responsibilities including childcare. The list should (1) name each responsibility, (2) briefly describe what must be done and when to accomplish it, (3) name the spouse that wants it accomplished and (4) how important is it to that spouse (use a scale from 1-5, with 1 least important and 5 most important).

Both spouses should work on this list, and it will take several days to cover the bases. You will add items each day as you find yourself accomplishing various tasks or wanting them accomplished.

Step 2: Assume responsibility for items that you would enjoy doing or prefer doing yourself.
Make a second copy of your final list, so that both you

and your wife can have your own copy. Then, independently of each other, put your own name in front of each item that you would like to do yourself. These are tasks that you would enjoy doing, don't mind doing, or want to do so they can be done a certain way.

When you compare your lists, if both you and your wife have named the same items, you can either take turns doing them, or arbitrarily divide them between the two of you. But you must approve each other's selections before they become your responsibilities.

Step 3: Assign the remaining responsibilities to the one wanting each done the most.
Assuming that all tasks you would not mind doing have been eliminated, we are left with those that would be unpleasant for either of you to perform. These are items that neither of you want to do, but at least one of you thinks it should be done.

These unpleasant responsibilities should be assigned to the person who wants them done. If both of you want something done the one giving it the highest value should take responsibility for doing it.

Step 4: Learn to help each other with your household responsibilities enthusiastically.

Up to this point, the assignment of household responsibilities is fair. You are dividing responsibilities according to willingness and according to who benefits most with their accomplishment.

But marriage takes you one step further. In marriage, you do things for each other because you care about each other's feelings, not just because you want them done yourself. You may not be willing to take responsibility for a certain task because, quite frankly, you don't think it needs to be done. But if your wife thinks it needs to be done, you will sometimes help her with it because you care for your wife.

RELATED SCRIPTURE:
1 Timothy 3:5
If anyone does not know how to manage his own family, how can he take care of God's church?

IF YOU REJECT THE ABOVE,
YOU WILL CREATE
THESE NEGATIVE CONSEQUENCES:
- She feels lonesome.
- She builds resentment toward you.
- She loses respect for your unwillingness to do hard, or "nitty-gritty" work at home.
- She feels like you are not proud of the family and the home.

Even though these objectives are ideals, it is important for husbands and wives to identify them as areas that need consistent work. It is natural to expect your mate to measure up to the above ideals by a certain time; however, nothing should be expected, except an attitude of appreciation for the progress made thus far.

QUESTIONS TO PONDER

1.   Do you feel that the lines of communication are fully open between you and each member of your family?

1 Thessalonians 2:8-12
So, affectionately longing for you, we were well pleased to impart to you not only the gospel of God, but also our own lives, because you had become dear to us. For you remember, brethren, our labor and toil; for laboring night and day, that we might not be a burden to any of you, we preached to you the gospel of God. You are witnesses, and God also, how devoutly and justly and blamelessly we behaved ourselves among you who believe; as you know how we exhorted, and comforted, and charged every one of you, as a father does his own children, that you would walk worthy of God who calls you into His own kingdom and glory.

2.   Does each member of your family know what your specific personal and family goals are?

James 1:22
But be doers of the word, and not hearers only, deceiving yourselves.

3.   Have you helped each member of your family set up clearly defined goals?

Short-Range And Long-Range Goals For The Development Of Inner Qualities And Outward Achievement

4.   Are you able to trace conflicts with your family to basic causes?

1 Corinthians 2:15-16
But he who is spiritual judges all things, yet, he himself is rightly judged by no one. For "who has known the mind of the Lord that he may instruct Him?" But we have the mind of Christ.

5.   Are you satisfied with your family's response to your authority? (Your family's attitude toward your authority has become their subconscious attitude towards the Lord's authority)

1 Timothy 1:16
However, for this reason I obtained mercy, that in me first Jesus Christ might show all longsuffering, as a pattern to those who are going to believe on Him for everlasting life.

6.   Are you respected by your family to the same degree that Jesus Christ is to be respected by the church?

Ephesians 5:23-33

For the husband is head of the wife, as also Christ is head of the church; and He is the Savior of the body. Therefore, just as the church is subject to Christ, so let the wives be to their own husbands in everything. Husbands, love your wives, just as Christ also loved the church and gave Himself for her, that He might sanctify and cleanse her with the washing of water by the word, that He might present her to Himself a glorious church, not having spot or wrinkle or any such thing, but that she should be holy and without blemish. So husbands ought to love their own wives as their own bodies; he who loves his wife loves himself. For no one ever hated his own flesh, but nourishes and cherishes it, just as the Lord does the church. For we are members of His body, of His flesh and of His bones. "For this reason a man shall leave his father and mother and be joined to his wife, and the two shall become one flesh." This is a great mystery, but I speak concerning Christ and the church. Nevertheless let each one of you in particular so love his own wife as himself, and let the wife see that she respects her husband.

7.   Are you actively interested in your children's activities, church, school, interests, etc?

Proverbs 20:5
Counsel in the heart of man is like deep water, But a man of understanding will draw it out.

Proverbs 27:19
As in water face reflects face, So a man's heart reveals the man.

8. Do you pray with the children as well as with your wife?

Ephesians 6:4
And you, fathers, do not provoke your children to wrath, but bring them up in the training and admonition of the Lord.

9. Do you plan outings for the children and create in them an interest for the really important things in life?

Ephesians 5:25
Husbands, love your wives, just as Christ also loved the church and gave Himself for her,

10. Do you have the freedom to share your deepest and fondest dreams with you wife?

11. Do you feel a freedom to share your areas

of weakness with your wife?

12. When your wife criticizes you, do you feel she has your best interest at heart?

13. Do you think your wife feels you have her best interest at heart?

14. Do you feel your wife appreciates you? Do you know why?

15. Do you get angry with your wife when she disagrees with you?

16. Do you understand the questions your wife is "really" asking from her heart in addition to what her mouth is saying?

17. Does your wife's attitude, words, or actions ever embarrass you in public?

18. Do you discuss with your wife new purchases that you want?

19. Regardless of the amount of income, does your wife feel secure in God's ability to supply the needs of the family through you?

20.   Do you find it difficult to control your temper during family conflicts?

Proverbs 13:10
By pride comes nothing but strife, But with the well-advised is wisdom.

Proverbs 15:1
A soft answer turns away wrath, But a harsh word stirs up anger.

James 4:1
Where do wars and fights come from among you? Do they not come from your desires for pleasure that war in your members?

21.   Do you make it a practice to verbally acknowledge to your family when you have been wrong? (Two most common complaints lodged against fathers are, a) they cannot control their temper, and b) out of pride, they rarely admit that they have been wrong)

James 5:16
Confess your trespasses to one another, and pray for one another, that you may be healed. The effective, fervent prayer of a righteous man avails much.

Matthew 5:24
...leave your gift there before the altar, and go your way. First be reconciled to your brother, and then come and offer your gift.

22.   Do you feel that you know how to apply basic scriptural principles in achieving lasting solutions for family conflicts? (In overcoming pride, anger worry, resentment, guilt, moral impurity, apathy, compromise, etc.)

23.   Are you fully aware of your role in the home?

Ephesians 5:25
Husbands, love your wives, just as Christ also loved the church and gave Himself for her,

24.   Is your testimony in your home one that you would be willing to share with anyone?

Proverbs 22:17-22
Incline your ear and hear the words of the wise, And apply your   heart to my knowledge; For it is a pleasant thing if you keep them within you; Let them all be fixed upon your lips, So that your trust may be in the Lord; I have instructed you today, even you. Have I not written to you excellent things of counsels

and knowledge, That I may make you know the certainty of the words of truth, that you may answer words of truth to those who send to you? Do not rob the poor because he is poor, nor oppress the afflicted at the gate.

ACKNOWLEDGMENTS

Thanks to all who typed, read, offered helpful
suggestions and edited this manuscript:
My wife, Tressie;
sister Lela Blue;
daughter, Jeana Stoddard;
granddaughter, Cassandra Jones;
friend, Zenitra Marginez;
and son, Robert White.

ABOUT
DR. LLOYD C. BLUE

HIS EDUCATION:
Doctor of Ministry
University of Central
America *
Kansas City, Missouri

Master of Arts
Union University *
Los Angeles, California

Bachelor of Theology
Institutional Baptist Theological Center *
Houston, Texas

HIS EXPERIENCE:
Senior Pastor in the **Baptist Denomination**
thirty-one (31) years.

Instructor/Lecturer with **Campus Crusade for
Christ International** teaching pastoral
management and personal evangelism for fifteen
years (15).

Founder/President of **Church Growth Unlimited, Inc.** for the past twenty-six (26) years.

Dr. Blue, known to many as a leading authority on church growth, was led of the Spirit to enter into full-time ministry as a consultant on church grown and he is responsible for the organization of **Church Growth Unlimited, Inc.**

He is both nationally and internationally acclaimed for his lectures in the areas of **Personal Evangelism, The Ministry of the Holy Spirit, Abundant Christian Living, Building Disciples, Church Growth, Family Enrichment, Pastoral Management, The Mechanics of Expository Preaching** and **How to Conduct City/Statewide Revivals.**

Dr. Blue has been the guest speaker for many National and International Christian organizations of many cultures, including:

The Annual Keswick Convention
Keswick, England
The Greenbelt Festival
South Shower, England
Here's Life Black America Conference
Nationwide

In Contact Ministries
London, England
The Nation Baptist Convention of America
Nationwide
The National Black Evangelical Association
Nationwide
The National Black Pastors Conference
Nationwide
The National Southern Baptist Convention
Nationwide

Dr. Blue is one of the most gifted and exciting preachers of the contemporary black church scene. His compelling understanding of the Gospel and its relationship to the complexities of our culture has made him one of the most requested lecturers of our day.

He is a native of **North Carolina**. He and his wife, **Tressie**, have been married fifty-five years and are the parents of one son, **Lloyd II**.

Also from Searchlight Press

The Way of Wisdom:
Job, Proverbs, Ecclesiastes,
Song of Solomon
translated by John Cunyus

Search the Scriptures:
A Step-By-Step Approach
to Deeper Spiritual Understanding
by Robert L. Dees

Character Is Key
by Eddie Hill and Dr. Jim Moore

Words Before Dawn
by Dr. Mack T. Flemmings

The Seventy Week Ministry
of Jesus Christ
by Michael Cotten

Searchlight Press
Who are you looking for?
Publishers of thoughtful Christian books since 1994.
5634 Ledgestone Drive
Dallas, TX 75214-2026
info@Searchlight-Press.com
www.Searchlight-Press.com

9 7 8 1 9 3 6 4 9 7 0 6 5